AF431801

The Role of the Moon for Woman of the Earth

By

Waikhom Bhumeswar Singh

The Role of the Moon for Woman of the Earth

Waikhom Bhumeswar Singh

First Edition, 2024
Self-Published

Contact:

bhumeswar.waikhom@gmail.com

Copyright © 2026 Waikhom Bhumeswar Singh
All rights reserved.

The views and opinions expressed in this book are solely those of the author. The facts and interpretations presented are based on the author's research, philosophical reflections, and personal understanding.

No part of this publication may be reproduced, stored in a retrieval system, or transmitted in any form or by any means—electronic, mechanical, photocopying, recording, or otherwise—without prior written permission from the author.

ACKNOWLEDGMENTS

I express my heartfelt gratitude to my family members, relatives, and friends who supported me at different stages of preparing this book, especially in drawing diagrams and illustrations.

I offer my reverence to the Almighty Lord, to my spiritual guides including Professor Dr. P. Ranbir Singh of DM College of Science, and to my beloved father, Late Waikhom Iboton Singh (Selungba), who served in the Manipur Kingdom during the reign of Maharaj Sir Churachand. He worked as a home tutor in the royal family and inspired me with a unique vision of life. From him, I learned to see human existence as a divine drama on the stage of the Earth, guided by the Sun and the Moon under the direction of the Lord.

The central philosophy of my writings reflects this understanding: that life moves in cycles, shaped by the rhythms of the Earth, the Sun, and the Moon. The balance of opposites, the changing seasons, and the union of man and woman are part of a larger divine order. Every individual plays a role in this cosmic drama, contributing to history for future generations.

I am grateful to Prof. Dr. Shanta Laishram, my son-in-law, for helping me submit documents digitally, and to many others who offered guidance and encouragement throughout this journey.

My sincere thanks to my family members for their constant support:

- Asst. Prof. Dr. Kabita Devi Waikhom (daughter)

- Er. Moirangthem Gautam Singh (son-in-law)

- Er. Waikhom Dhaneswar Singh (son)

- Er. Waikhom Khelchandra Singh

- Er. Waikhom Ningsuhen (nephew)

- Er. Akoijam Gyanandari Devi

I also remember with respect those who gave me opportunities to learn and grow through discussion and experience.

The illustrations in this book were prepared with assistance from my family members. Some reference images were collected for educational purposes, and several diagrams were specially drawn under my direction to support the ideas presented.

Despite challenges and criticism, I remained committed to completing this work as a humble service to the Lord. I remain deeply thankful to everyone who stood beside me in this journey.

INTRODUCTION

This book explores the relationship between the Earth, the Moon, and the Sun as governing forces of life. It presents the view that the cycles of nature are not random movements in space, but structured patterns that influence life, growth, reproduction, and human responsibility.

The Earth revolves around the Sun while rotating on its axis, inclined between the Northern and Southern hemispheres. This movement gives rise to solstices and equinoxes, creating seasonal cycles of summer and winter, spring and autumn. Within this system, the Moon orbits the Earth, generating new moon and full moon phases that interact with gravitational and magnetic forces.

According to the perspective presented in this book, these cosmic cycles shape not only environmental conditions but also the rhythm of life itself. The alternation between solstice and equinox, and between new moon and full moon, forms a structured pattern of time divided into quarters. These quarters correspond to periods of growth, maturity, rest, and renewal.

The author proposes that the Northern and Southern hemispheres function as complementary halves of a unified whole. Just as day and night balance each other, so do summer and winter, sunrise and sunset, attraction and repulsion, positive and negative magnetic forces. This balance is reflected in the relationship between man and woman, which is viewed as a natural extension of the Earth–Moon partnership.

In this framework, spring and autumn are seen as particularly significant transitional periods following the solstices and leading toward the equinoxes. These seasons represent renewal and preparation within the larger cycle of nature. The full moon and new moon phases are interpreted as moments of intensified interaction between the Earth and the Moon, symbolizing deeper natural processes at work.

While there are many religions and cultures across the world, this work suggests that the underlying principles of life are governed by one universal order expressed through natural law. The Sun and the Moon, in their movements, project forces that influence the living organisms of the Earth. The harmony of life depends upon understanding and respecting these cycles.

This book seeks to integrate spiritual philosophy with scientific observation. It invites readers to reflect on how cosmic order relates to human conduct, family life, and social responsibility. By aligning human life with the structured rhythms of the Earth and the Moon, the author argues that society can move toward greater balance, peace, and continuity across generations.

The purpose of this work is not merely to describe astronomical phenomena, but to encourage a disciplined understanding of time, nature, and duty. Through awareness of these cycles, humankind may better fulfill its role within the greater system of the universe.

"TERMS AND DIAGRAMS" FOR READING THE BOOK

Solstice: longest day & night of summer & winter on north & south fix in the 21st/22nd June and 22nd/23rd December six monthly quite opposite on North & South and quite opposite from East & West according to the position of axis of the Earth & Moon around Sun.

That solstice falls on the 21st/22nd June and 22nd/23rd December quite opposite on the Earth's north & south axis at 23" latitude from line of equator as tropic of Cancer & tropic of Capricorn six monthly as up & down journey of the Earth. The Earth's Axis inclines to the Northeast & Southeast after every solstice of June by 23° on north & December on south by 23° from the equator line of March and September as up journey and down journey due to inclination quite opposite on north & south six monthly from solstice to solstice and from equinox to equinox. But quarterly from solstice to equinox and from equinox to solstice quite opposite on north to south. Life cycles of super human beings of male & female of opposite halves begin after summer/winter solstice of north & south clockwise &

anticlockwise. The summer of either half is for animal kind of land & water. The first quarter of winter is for receiving fruits of Lord before solstice and the second quarter of winter is after solstice as spring/autumn of either half for boarding live cells of the Sun & the Moon as agents of the Lord into eggs of Mother Earth/Moon.

The north and south fields of the earth around the sun axis is for every six months from north to south (clockwise) and from south to north (anti clockwise) as morning and evening hours of the year quite opposite on north and south.

The time cycles opposite halves meet at midnight at the end of evening but at the beginning of morning moonlight system of the lord during full moon week at 00.00 hrs. in the west sky and there is end of morning 12.00 hrs. at noon and of evening 12.00 hrs. at midnight.

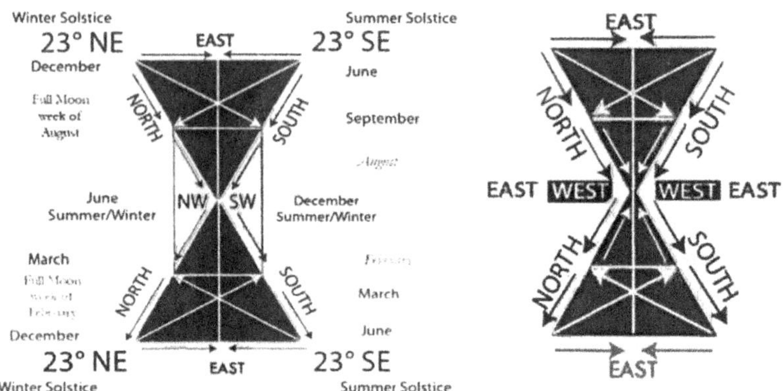

Diagram 3 : Unit of Opposite halves of the earth is formed by the opposite fields of the Earth & the Moon before equinox. The crossing line before September is in the August month for meeting two halves.

The crossing line before March is in the February.

Equinox: The shortest equal day & night of summer & winter that falls on the $21^{st}/22^{nd}$ March and $22^{nd}/23^{rd}$ September on the Earth quite opposite on north & south of winter & summer on the line of equator according to positions of the Earth & the Moon around Sun as up and down journey.

Summer: The Earth's opposite field facing to the Sun

for every six months.

Winter: The Earth's opposite field are quite opposite to the Sun & the Moon as new moon & full moon for every six months.

Perigee & Apogee is distance of the Moon from the Earth at new moon & full moon in a particular month of solar calendar from January to December. Primary position of the Moon as Perigee & Apogee in a particular month of January to December returns after eighteen years after completing the journey of solar system in the orbit around Black hole of the Galaxy of the Universe.

Extra additional lunar month increase in every 33 to 36 lunar months "as mono mass" regulated by the time cycle of solstice & equinox of the year.

Extra additional day of day & night increase in every four years as leap year according to positions of the Earth & the Moon in February and August month as spring & autumn of winter & summer of either half of North or South.

The North & South field of the Earth's axis relate to the positive & negative field of magnetic bar of the mass body of the Earth as male & female organism of the Earth projected by the positive & negative fields of the Sun & the Moon according to the cycle of rotation & revolution of the Earth & Moon around Sun's axis of North & South that begins after every solstice of summer & winter quite the opposite on north & south of the Earth.

Relationship of the Earth & Moon in the journey orbiting around Sun's axis of North & South field relates to the relationship of man & woman as life partner for planning to produce the best offspring of the Earth & the Moon in spring & autumn as issues of the Lord for the welfare of every family of any community at any region of the Earth.

The autumn is the spring of either field of North or South, so, every parent should install the XY cells of the Sun & Moon into XX live cells of waterbody into eggs of woman mother Earth in spring of either half so that the best offspring can mature in autumn of either spring to get the real issue of the Lord for the welfare of every family of any people on the Earth.

The best offspring of the Earth & Moon is the spring & autumn babies of humankind as issues of the Lord projected by the Sun & Moon in the solar system in time.

ABOUT THE AUTHOR

Waikhom Bhumeswar Singh was born in 1949, in the years following India's independence and prior to the merger of Manipur with India. He is the fifth son of Late Shree Waikhom Iboton @ Shelungba Singh, a matriculate of 1923 who served in the Revenue Department of the erstwhile Kingdom of Manipur during the reign of Sir Churachand Maharaj. His father also worked as a tutor in the royal household and was a descendant of Maharaj Devendra of Manipur (reigned 1857).

His mother, Haobam Ningol Ibemcha Devi, was the eldest daughter of Haobam Guru Atomba Singh, a renowned dance Guru and Padma Shri awardee of Uripok Haobam Dewan Leikai.

Raised under strong moral and spiritual guidance, he was deeply influenced by his father's teachings. He grew up with the belief that humankind is created to face life's challenges with integrity and faith, that suffering arises from one's own actions, and that fulfilment depends on the sincere discharge of duty in harmony with divine and natural principles.

He completed Class XI under the Delhi Board in 1968, studying civics, economics, geography, mathematics, general science, and Hindi. He earned his Bachelor of Arts degree in Geography, English, and Manipuri Political Science from Guwahati University in 1971–72, and later obtained his LLB degree from Lucknow University in 1975, securing First Class.

He practiced as a private lawyer and was registered with the Guwahati High Court from 1976 to 1979.

In 1978, he was appointed Assistant Public Prosecutor (APP) by the Manipur Public Service Commission. After revision of the pay scale, he joined government service in 1979 in the higher grade. In February 1984, he was appointed Public Prosecutor in the Central Bureau of Investigation (CBI) for the Northeast region by the Union Public Service Commission. After six years of service, he was selected for promotion as Senior Public Prosecutor in February 1991. He declined the promotion and resigned in March 1991 to dedicate himself to the care and education of his young children in Imphal.

He later served as Additional Public Prosecutor-cum-Additional Government Advocate in the State of Manipur from 1991 until

December 1999. He voluntarily retired from government service to devote himself to writing and social service.

Beyond his legal profession, he has been actively involved in social and international initiatives. In 2000, he joined the Indo Japan Friendship International Organization and served as General Secretary for Manipur. He also worked as a social worker with the Grievances Relief Organisation Manipur. In August 2001, he participated in the Fifth World Conference of Mayors for Peace in Hiroshima and Nagasaki, Japan, where he delivered a speech addressing poverty eradication and environmental responsibility through spiritual and scientific principles.

In 2003, he became a Charter Member of the Lions Club of Canchipur under District 322D. He served in various leadership roles including Secretary, President, District Chairperson, and Zone Chairperson. In 2007, he donated land in collaboration with a fellow member for the construction of the Lions Club Canchipur Centre Building. The structure was completed with RCC roofing in 2019–20 and formally handed over to the club in 2020–21.

As an independent thinker and researcher, Waikhom Bhumeswar Singh has authored several works exploring the relationship between cosmic order and human life. His writings seek to integrate spiritual philosophy with scientific observation, focusing on the Earth, the Moon, and the Sun as governing forces of life cycles.

His published works include:

The Secrets of Life (November 2002)

The Calendar of Life Cycles for Century (December 2002)

The Great Book of the Earth & the Moon, Volume II (August 2022; revised 2023/24)

The Great Book of the Environment of the Earth, Volume I

The Relationship of the Earth & Moon as the Relationship of Man and Woman

The Role of the Moon for Woman of the Earth

Through his writings, he seeks to present a systematic understanding of natural law, encouraging humanity to live responsibly and in harmony with the cycles of the Earth and the Moon.

List of Contents

CHAPTER 1

Role of Woman on the Earth as directed by Goddess Mother Moon.

The role of Moon Goddess is the role of Goddess Mother Earth (Woman), and every Woman takes the role of Moon Goddess and the great Goddess Mother Earth takes the role of Woman mother in every family for growing humankind of the Earth's opposite halves for reproducing living cells of opposite organism of life plants of the Earth:- Every woman follows the cycle of the Moon orbiting around the Earth's axis of north & south and every woman like   the Moon follows recycles of rotation and revolution of the

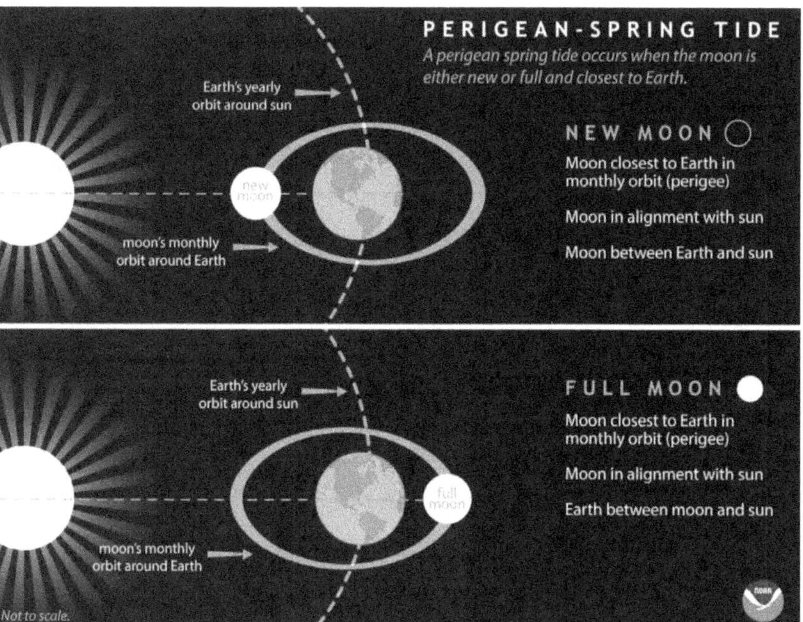

Earth orbiting around the Sun's axis after the solstice of December and June.

Position of the Earth and Moon after every Solstice for recycle. The Moon follows the speed of the Earth orbiting around the Sun for reproduction living cells of waterbody in the pot of Mother Earth (Woman). Every Woman reproduces living cells of waterbody in the living pot of Goddess Mother Earth for growing living XY & XX cells energy of senses of plus and minus of Humankind of the Lord during full Moon week when the Earth's axis is in between the Sun & the Moon. The opposite fields of the Sun & the Moon charge two times in the 1st & 3rd quarter of year quite opposite on north & south as spring & autumn for the people of the world settled on the Earth's northern and southern hemispheres.

Therefore, every Woman mother must take the role of Goddess Mother Earth and the Moon Goddess as life partner. The earth/moon contribute attractive (Negative) magnetic force during full Moon week on the Earth's opposite fields as spring & autumn seasons in the 1st & 3rd quarter of year for installation of living energy of senses of the Lord for humankind of the earth in the living alive life- pots of great Mother Earth/ Moon on north & south (woman mother) at midnight hour of winter/summer during full moon week for utilization of the eggs of new life plants produced in spring & autumn seasons. The conceived babies can grow properly in the 2nd & 4th quarter of year:

CHAPTER 2

Position of Earth & Moon after Solstice

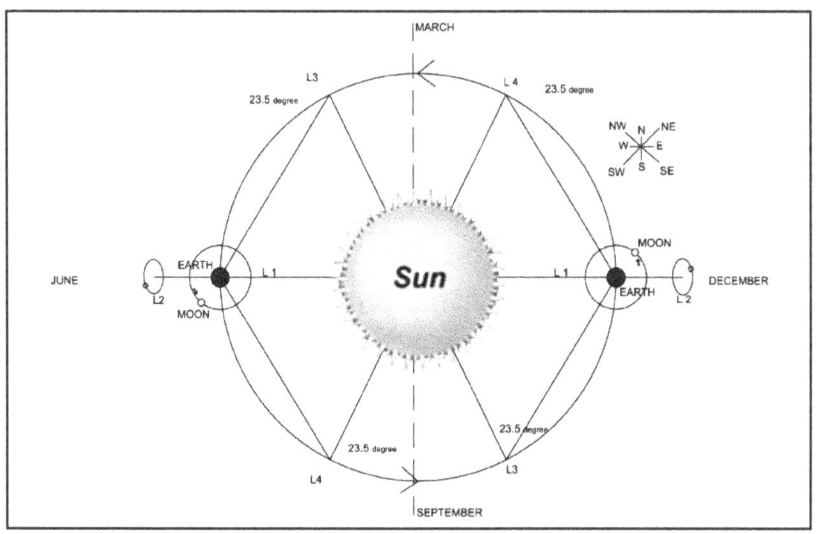

Position of Earth & Moon after Solstice of December & June

The Woman mother is producing eggs of (negative) magnetic force on the Earth's axis quite opposite to the Sun at midnight winter/ summer according to the position of the

Earth/ Moon around the Sun God to the North & south after solstice lunar monthly for three months as spring & autumn before equinox, after equinox the earth/ moon change their respective position from north to south and from south to north from equator line. That is from summer to winter and from winter to summer after every spring & autumn after every equinox. After equinox, the earth's one half crossing towards summer cannot cross the equatorial line towards solstice. This period of summer of up journey is for production of life cycles of animal kind of land/ water of animal instinct. But the opposite field of the Earth is down journey for releasing living beings of humanity of humankind and associate living beings/plants. Every Woman mother has power to utilize the role of great Goddess Mother Moon of the Earth at midnight winter/ summer during full Moon week in the morning hour of the local time. So, every big country should divide local time of the state to administer the people & living beings of the environment properly as directed by the Lord.

Like the Moon Goddess reflects Sunlight as new moon period in summer and as full Moon period in winter on the Earth's opposite halves after solstice as autumn /spring on opposite fields. The Sun & the Moon contribute extra energy of light system as repulsive forces in the evening moonlight in the new moon period as impulsive with gravitational forces on the Earth's opposite fields when the eath's axis is in between the Sun & the Earth. The Earth & the Moon also produce extra impulsive forces on the Earth's opposite fields to enlighten the humankind on the Earth after solstice as spring towards summer and as autumn towards winter during prolonged daytime & nighttime on the Earth's opposite fields with slanting light system of the Lord remove the dark shadow in the Pole region of either half of north or south before equinox.

But after the equinox of north & south equal short daytime & nighttime, the Earth's axis of either north or south, the light system of the Lord cannot contribute the slanting moonlight towards the Pole region of either north or south as the Earth & the Moon are in the equatorial regions of the Sun & the Earth. This period of summer of up journey of north or south is reserved for animal kind of animal instinct in the land / water. The Divine life ancestors of Manipuri people reserve this lunar month as "shajibu tha". "Sha" = animal kind, "Jiba" = living beings/plants.

Every woman mother of the Earth is living in a family as mother "laxmi" & as creator "Naran" of the earth/ moon. Every man & woman as life partner of the Lord should select the autumn & spring seasons of the light system of the Lord to reflect the autumn Sunlight as morning Moonlight of spring with seven senses of rainbow on the Earth's opposite fields at midnight with Negative magnetic fields quite opposite to the Sun. The above diagram of two ends shows the new moon as red color autumn for charging two opposite fields for beginning the new moon period. The green period is the full Moon week of the Earth's opposite fields. The full moon week are occurred on north or south when the Earth is in between the Sun & the Moon.

Because of the positions of the Earth & the Moon around the Sun's axis after solstice the Earth & the Moon install live cells of the Lord for creation of human life plants of the earth/moon into living cells of waterbody contained in the eggs of the mother earth/moon in the living alive life- pots of Goddess Mother Earth (Woman) on north & south in the 1st quarter and again in the 3rd quarter of year to to grow in the 2nd quarter of year summer/ winter and to complete the process in the 3rd quarter of year and again to grow in the 4th quarter of year summer/ winter and to complete the process in the 1st quarter of year quite opposite on the north & south of the Earth.

Every woman produces living cells of waterbody as eggs from the right & left ovaries in the living alive life-pots of the great Woman Mother Earth on north & south with Negative magnetic fields of the Sun & the Moon for growing living energy of senses of the Sun God & the Moon Goddess in the life-pots of the Goddess Mother of the Earth/ Moon.

When the Woman fulfils the object of installation living energy of seven senses of the Sun and the Moon from the East & from West at midnight winter/summer into living cells of waterbody in the life-pots of great Goddess Mother Earth/ Moon in time as projected by the Sun and the Moon during full Moon week when the magnetic fields of the Earth & the Moon are active. In the matter of reproduction of issues of the Lord on the stage of the Earth we parent of the Earth's opposite fields are bound to follow the principles of the Lord for the welfare of every member in a family and in the clan of the family of humankind that comes from generation to generations under certain principle of the Earth /Moon.

CHAPTER 3

New Moon and Full Moon Period of the Earth's Opposite Axis

comes after every Solstice.

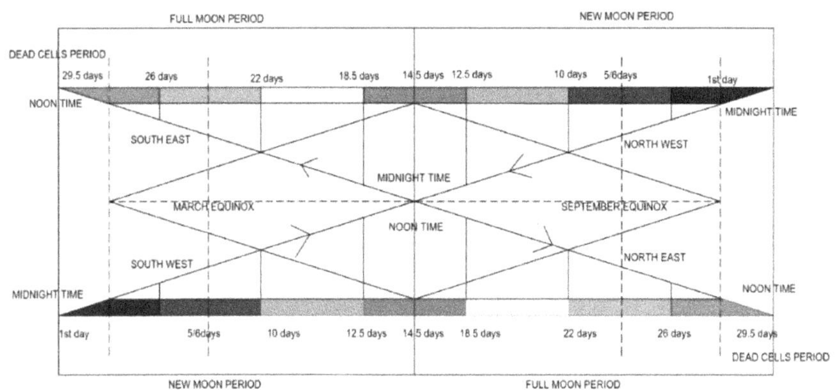

New Moon and Full Moon Period is quite opposite on Northern and Southern Hemisphere

The above diagram shows the life cycles of north and south according to new moon period of north and full Moon period south distributed after solstice lunar monthly for six months as spring & autumn quarterly and as summer & winter quarterly quite opposite on north clockwise and on south anticlockwise as part of morning and as part of evening hours of six months of year.

That is the diagram showing the life cycles of Humankind and other living beings/ plants of opposite halves of the Earth's north & south following timescale of morning moonlight /sunlight and evening sunlight system of six months of year. The Sun & the Moon project winter/ summer at midnight as morning light system of year and

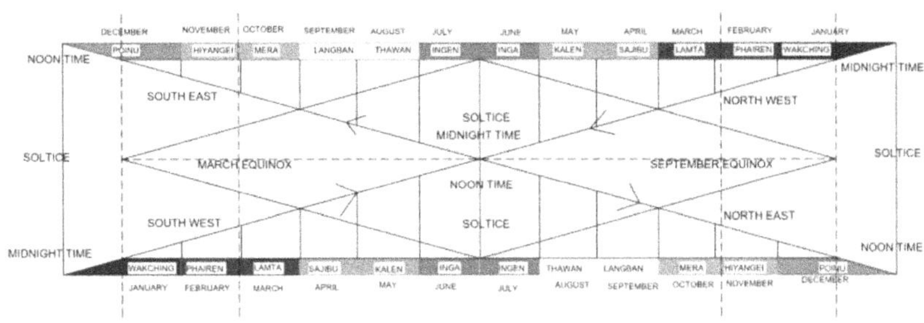

Light cycle of the Sun and Moon around the Earth begins after
December solstice (clockwise) on north for six months and after
June solstice (anti-clockwise) on south for six months.

noontime as summer/winter six monthly quite opposite on north & south after every solstice. Life cycles of male & female begins after December solstice and after solstice of June solstice to complete the growing process of opposite halves from the longest daytime & nighttime of the year. But January of the 1st quarter of year and July of the 3rd quarter of year is setting period but for beginning of new life cycles of life system of the Earth's opposite fields must begin around February and around August during full moon week at midnight of winter/summer of either half.

Every individual of opposite halves as a member of the opposite fields. But every parent are agent of the Earth's opposite fields united as whole body system of the Earth/Moon projected by the

Lord. So, every couple is a common plan of the Lord to form a family life partners of the earth's opposite axis charged by the opposite fields of the Sun & the Moon after solstice of summer & winter as autumn & spring of opposite halves. So, every man & woman are grown up life partner developed under the course of life cycles of the Earth & the Moon projected by the Sun & the Moon along with other planets of the solar system. In this age of advanced science & technology, we human life plants of opposite fields must educate the system principles of the recycles rotation / revolution of the Earth & the Moon projected by the opposite fields of the Sun & the Moon after solstice into eggs of north & south in the alive lifeboats of male & female in the right & left ovaries of the goddess woman mother of the earth/moon projected by the Sun & the Moon after solstice of summer/winter as new moon period of two weeks for developing XY cells to the man /male of the Earth and XX cells into eggs of Goddess Mother of the Earth/ Moon developed into eggs of woman & female mother of the earth/moon in spring and autumn quarterly before equinox of north & south and after equinox of north & south as summer in up journey and as winter in the down journey.

Considering the above facts & figures of the earth/ moons positions after solstice and after equinox quarterly, every family life partner must have a well- organized family planning to form a unit of lifeboats of male & female of human society to sail the lifeboats of north & south of Godfather and Goddess Mother of the Earth's opposite hemisphere properly before equinox of north & south to sail on opposite directions towards solstice and after solstice towards equinox as shown in the above diagram as projected by the Sun God & the Moon Goddess as issues of Nature. Every family life partner must select the right time scale of morning & evening hours of year of rotation /revolution of the Earth & the Moon around the Sun. It is bounden duty of every parent to select the right timescale of the Lord for the welfare of future younger generations.

We must know the spiritual & scientific systematic principles of creation of humankind and associated other life plants of light system with impulsive magnetic force of the Sun & the Moon in the living life pot of great Mother Earth (Woman) as projected by the opposite magnetic fields of the Sun and the Moon at midnight during full Moon week (from 12th to 18th days) (I) in the 1st quarter of year as spring of winter on the Northern half and as autumn of summer on Southern half after

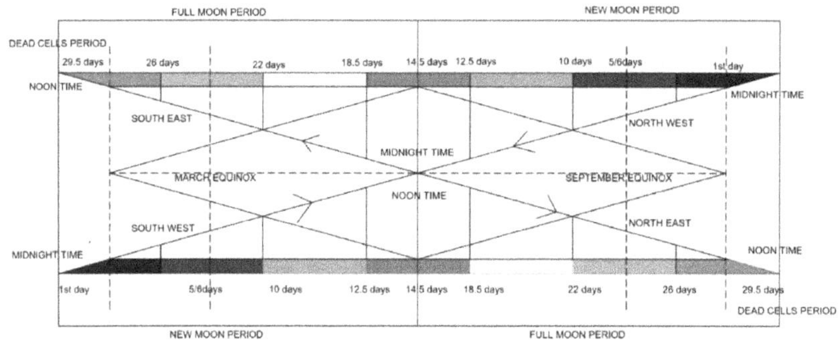

LIFE CYCLES OF OPPOSITE HALVES

New moon and Full moon period are quite opposite

on Northern and Southern Hemisphere after every solstice

winter solstice and (II) in the 3rd quarter as spring of winter on Southern half and as autumn of summer on Northern half. If we select to follow the right morning & evening six months of a year clockwise on North and anticlockwise on the South. It is sure that the new life cycles of humankind would be the issues of the Earth/ Moon to release after 3rd quarter of year in the beginning of 4th quarter of the year on the North and to release after 2st quarter in the beginning of 2nd quarter of year on the South quite the opposite on north & south.

Every family life partner must consider very seriously about the principle & process of creation of humankind life plants of the Earth/Moon projected by light system with impulsive magnetic fields of the Sun and the Moon during full Moon week at midnight on the Earth by way of installation of living cells energy of the Lord in the living life pot of great Mother Earth (Woman) in the 1st quarter and 3rd quarter in spring of either half & to complete the growth in 3rd or 1st quarter of year quite opposite on north & south and to release the new plant in the 4th & 2nd quarter respectively after nine months in every year on the Earth.

This is the recorded data of accounts of humankind life plant as history for replantation, growing and reproduction of new life plants of the Earth's north & south in the life-pots of great earth/ moon as maintained by well-organized family of humankind under spiritual & scientific creative principles of the Earth/ Moon. This secret principle of creation of new life generation in the royal family in Manipur were maintained by the king & queens in the region of Manipur of the Earth. The king & queen of the Earth / Moon are ruled by the Sun God & the Moon Goddess to maintain the value of king & queen of the people of Manipur. An individual is the subject of the king & queen of the Earth's opposite fields.

The light cycle after solstice of June in Southern Hemisphere

The light cycle after solstice of December in Northern Hemisphere (Clockwise)

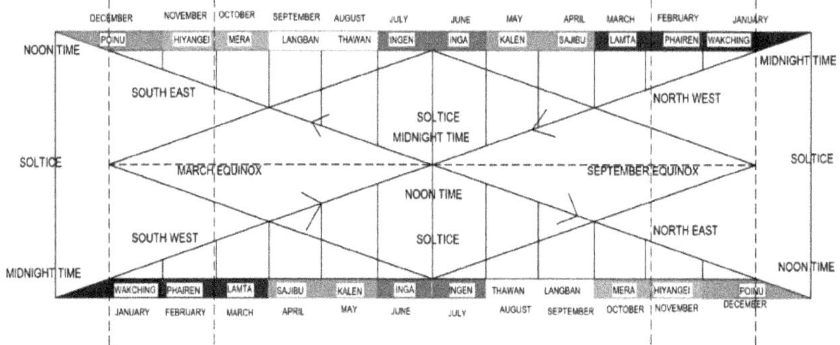

CHAPTER 4

The right and the wrong principles of life system of the Earth fixed by the Sun and the Moon

On the other hand, there are many numerous couples in Human society who destroy their own family members as they play against the spiritual & scientific recycles of the rotation/ revolutions of the Earth / Moon around the Sun. The parent who does not know the spiritual, and scientific creative principles of the Earth/ Moon regulated by the Lord are against the spiritual couple life and responsible family life partner of the Earth's north & south. Organized family are performing marriage ceremony in time unlike animal kind by performing spiritual norms in the society to maintain the spiritual and scientific principle of relationship of the Earth & the Moon at midnight during full moon week of winter/ summer for creation of new life plants generation on the Earth as projected by the Sun and the Moon. The Sun & the Moon produce opposite magnetic force on the Earth's axis for organized family life partner: - (I) The 1st quarter, is to grow in 2nd & to mature in the 3rd quarter and to deliver the offspring in the beginning of 4th quarter and (II) The 3rd quarter is also spring to form lifeboats of male & female to grow in the 4th & to mature in the 1st quarter for delivering the offspring in 2nd quarter in April according to the recycle of the Earth & the Moon around Sun's axis.

Solar Declination of Northern & Southern Hemisphere

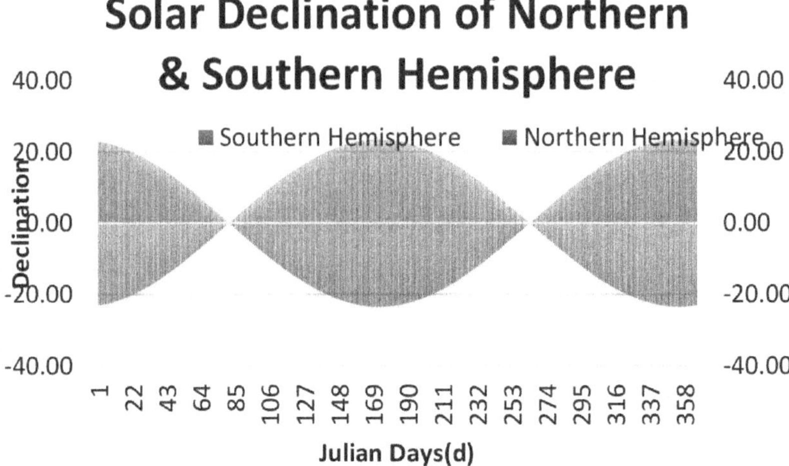

Intercrossing the light cycle of opposite halves
on the day of equinox of March & September on North & South.

According to declination of the opposite hemispheres on the day of equinox of March of northern hemisphere and on the day of equinox of September of southern hemisphere of equal shortest day & night of year the opposite fields enter crossing after every equinox within the line of equatorial region in the up-journey due to inclination of the Earth's axis. The line of equator of the Earth immediately decline towards the longer nighttime of winter of North & south of solstice of winter that occur quite opposite on north and south on the 22nd day of June and again on the day 22nd day of December of nature. Therefore, the solstice of either north or south axis of winter are over the pole regions before & after every solstice for reproduction the best offspring of the Earth. So, for new life cycles of the Earth's opposite hemisphere occur after winter solstice for three lunar months fixed after solstice to equinox of 21st March on north and after solstice to equinox before equinox of 22nd September on south.

So, every parent of humankind must install live cells of XY of the Lord into XX cells of the Earth/ Moon in spring of either north or south in order to grow in summer and to complete the growing process of new life cycles in the 3rd quarter or in the 1st quarter of year to release the offspring opposite fields as new life generation in the 4th or in the 2nd quarter of year.

Every citizen and every parent of the Earth /Moon as family life partner is responsible to aware the principle of opposite magnetic forces of the Earth's of North and South projected by the Sun and Moon on the Earth when the Earth is in between the Sun & the Moon at midnight winter/summer in the life journey around the North of the Sun before 22nd September and around the south of the Sun before the 21st March. Therefore, every lifeboat of man & woman is compulsory to sail from March to September and from September to March without any disturbance during the journey of human life according to recycle of the Earth & Moon after solstice to solstice after equinox to equinox around the Sun.

Everybody must know the fact & figures of human life as philosophic living beings/ plants of the Earth's opposite fields charged by the magnetic fields of the Sun and the Moon after every solstice on the Earth's opposite halves for planting XY cells of the Sun & the Moon into X living cells of waterbody contained into eggs as alive life-pots of Goddess Woman Mother produced from right & left ovaries of the Earth /Moon on north & south as projected by the Sun and the Moon during full Moon week (within 12th to 18th lunar days) in the 1st and 3rd quarter of year are up & down journey from solstice to solstice on north & south for six months to reproduce the new life generations of the Earths opposite haves.

Life cycles of human beings are from spring to autumn and autumn to spring to complete the process of opposite halves from autumn to equinox to produce offspring of north & south around equinox in 4th and in 2nd quarter of the year when the Earth/ Moon are in down journey from North to South and from south to north of the equatorial line of the Sun & the Earth.

Every family should know the systematic spiritual and scientific creative principles produced by the recycles of the Earth and the Moon around the Sun to the North six months and to the South six months after every solstice on north in June and on south in December. The creation of humankind by the opposite magnetic fields of the Sun and the Moon is during full Moon week (period) under certain principles of the Earth & the Moon as divine life process to be executed by every couple as a family life partners of the Earth & the Moon spiritually, and scientifically.

This is supported with human conscience on the Earth (from 12th to 18th day), of the lunar month of three months as spring & autumn quite opposite on north & south and east & west quite opposite to the Sun.

The period from 23rd December to 21st March and from 22nd June to 22nd September are subject to full Moon week. The installation of new energy of seven senses of live cells of the Lord into living alive life-pots of Goddess Mother Earth/Moon (Woman) is in the spring season in the 1st & 3rd quarter of year before equinox on north & south. The germinated live cells grow in the 2nd and 4th quarter on north and south to mature in the 3rd and 1st quarter of year to deliver the offspring just after equinox in the 4th and 2nd quarter of year as entrusted to humankind as "Pakhangba" in a year for the welfare of people and environment of the Earth.

Everybody must realize the spiritual and scientific magnetic fields of north and South Poles of the Earth projected by the Sun and the Moon around the Earth: -

That, every humankind life plant grows into living cells of waterbody of great Mother Earth/Moon as a product of opposite magnetic force of the Sun and the Moon on the Earth during the full Moon week period in spring of either half of the Earth quite the opposite to the Sun's axis.

That, the family life partners of people are live energy of the Earth and the Moon and can produce spiritual opposite magnetic force of the Sun and the Moon on the Earth as mature plants in the evening of year as per order of nature just after solstice 22nd /23rd December and 21st /22nd June as spring & autumn and as autumn & spring for production of humankind. The life partners of humankind must install spiritual energy of the Earth /Moon projected by the Lord during full Moon week at midnight in the living alive life-pots of great Mother Earth/ Moon in spring & autumn seasons of either field of the Earth when the family of the Earth & the Moon is to the North or south around Sun six months after solstice. The spring is from solstice of June to equinox of September and from solstice of December to equinox of March to germinate in the lifeboat and sail the lifeboats of male & female around the Sun in the ocean of life in the space.

The new moon and full moon occurs quite opposite after solstice of December & June on North & South.

That, the turning point of a year falls on the 22nd of December on the Earth's north on one side and again on the 22nd of June on Earth's south towards opposite fields passing equator of the Sun. The solstice of winter is the longest nighttime of the Earth for formation of new life plants cycle of the Earth starting from 23rd

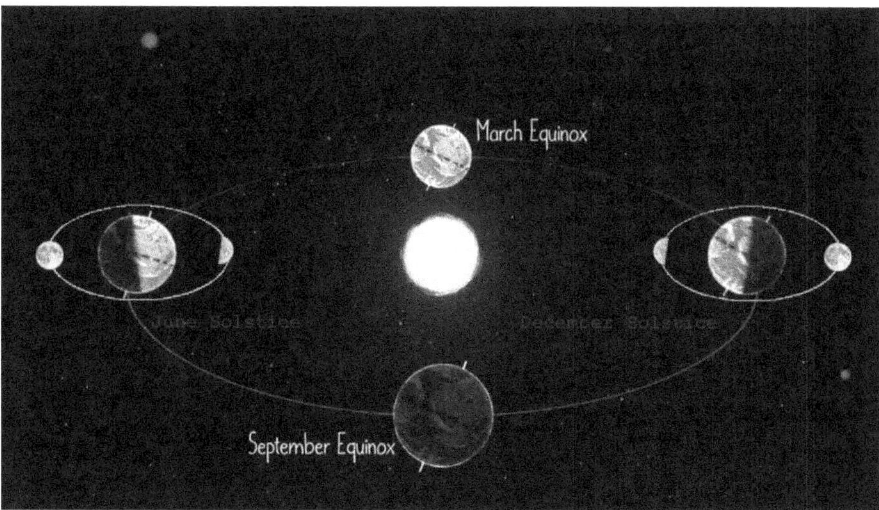

December to 21st March and from 22nd June to 22nd September subject to new moon and full Moon cycle around Earth's axis as new moon period of summer and as full Moon period of winter towards summer quite the opposite on north & south to the Sun's axis. The projection opposite magnetic fields of the Earth's axis occur at midnight winter/ summer during full Moon week when the earth is in between the Sun and the Moon.

Everybody must realize that there are repulsive magnetic fields of South Poles of the Earth around South Poles of the Sun and Moon during new Moon period from midday summer to midnight winter before equinox. The period after equinox of 21st /22nd March towards solstice of 21st June on the Northern half as summer clockwise and on the Southern half as winter anticlockwise. The summer period is up journey for growing living cells of life plants developed in the living life pots of great Mother Earth in the evening hours during repulsive forces and in the morning hours during impulsive magnetic force of the Moon around Earth's equatorial region. The repulsive magnetic fields of the Moon at noontime summer/winter as new moon period as evening hours out of six months of year and impulsive magnetic forces in the morning hours from midnight winter on opposite halves are not strong because of positions of the Earth & the Moon in the equatorial region of the Sun. At midnight winter as the full Moon period there is morning hours from midnight winter/summer towards midday summer /winter towards solstice. The summer & winter after equinox on opposite halves is for releasing mature life plants as offspring from the living life pots of great Mother Earth /Moon for animal kind as per short repulsive magnetic fields of the Sun & the Moon around Earth in the evening of year.

Quite opposite to Northern half the period from 23rd September to

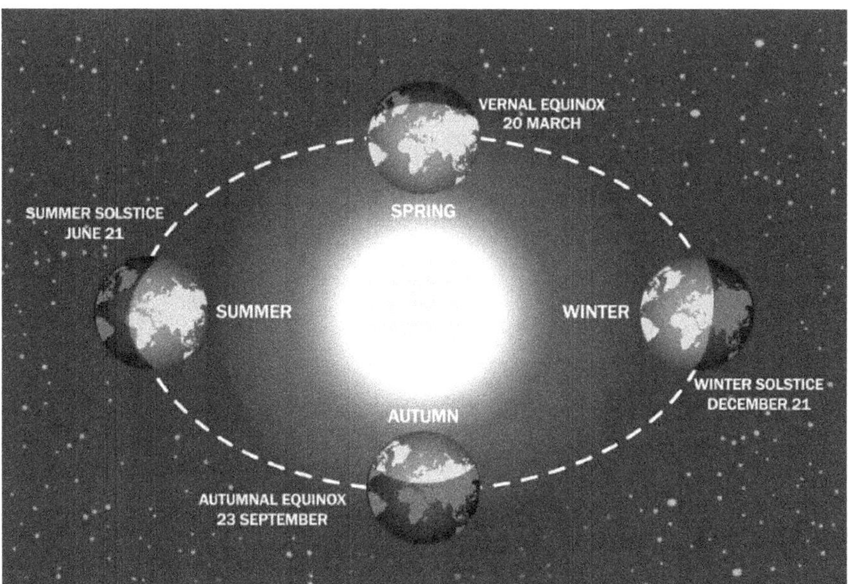

22nd December there is repulsive magnetic fields of the North of the Earth to the North fields of the Sun & Moon during new Moon period from noontime summer towards midnight winter. During new moon period, there is repulsive around the Earth in the evening hours and there are impulsive forces from midnight winter/summer to noontime summer/ winter. The first repulsive

& impulsive forces around the Earth's North & South fields are developed after solstice to equinox for humankind and the second repulsive & impulsive forces are developed from equinox to solstice during new moon period and full Moon period for animal kind of different varieties of land & water.

The spring & autumn of north & south is purely after solstice to equinox of March & September as spring & autumn on opposite fields facing to the Sun & the Moon during daytime and nighttime due to the positions of the earth /moon around the Sun. The summer & winter are after equinox of March on north and after equinox of September on south. The above picture of declination of the north & south fields after solstice as spring & autumn and after equinox of north & south as summer & winter quite the opposite on north & south hemispheres.

The Goddess Mother comes on the Earth in the month of October on north and in the month of April on south for maintaining peace & harmony life plants of opposite halves according to the Moon's cycle as new moon period from summer to winter and as full moon period from winter to summer on the Earth's opposite fields quite the opposite on the north & south for the welfare of humankind and other living beings on opposite halves for peace.

Therefore, the summer period is for growth of living cells of the Earth's on north & south half for growth, life plants in the living life pot of great Mother Moon of the Earth, after equinox on the Southern half in September and after equinox on Northern half in March are for releasing mature life plants as offspring of north & south as male & female just after equinox in winter.

When the family of the Earth and the Moon are towards the South of the Sun. The Sun contributes attractive (negative) magnetic force from Southern half towards Northern half of the Earth. The full Moon period of winter are for attractive forces of two opposite organisms of opposite halves during mature moon.

The growth of live cells of opposite fields of the Earth & Moon are carried by men & women for humankind and other male & female living beings/ plants of different varieties during mature moon week for reproduction living beings/ plants for growing into living cells of waterbody of the Earth/ Moon on north & south life pots according to the position of the Earth and the Moon around the Sun's axis of north & south six monthlies.

After equinox March & after equinox of September during full Moon period, the Moon contributes positive magnetic force quite opposite to the Sun around the Earth's opposite axis from the Sun and the Moon into living cells of waterbody in the pot of Goddess Mother the Earth & the Moon for growing life plants of animal kind and other living beings of the land /water to support humankind life plants growing in the life-'pots of great Mother Earth/Moon (Woman) and other female mothers.

The End of December and the end of June is a turning point of the whole-body system of the Earth's opposite halves to form life cycles of opposite organisms of the Earth's opposite halves within nine to ten lunar months out of six months of morning & evening hours of year divided (i) by the solstice of north & south as spring & autumn as morning & evening moonlight system quarterly and (ii) by the equinox of north & south as summer morning hours & as winter of evening hours quite opposite on north & south quarterly towards solstice.

The beginning of morning summer ends at noon & the beginning winter ends at midnight of the day & night occur towards solstice of the 21st / 22nd June. After solstice June, new life cycles of the Earth's opposite fields begin towards equinox of September as autumn of evening hours of summer and as spring of morning hours of winter subject to new moon period of summer and subject to full moon period winter before equinox of September. After equinox of September to December solstice is another beginning of summer and beginning of winter. As stated above morning summer is beginning animal kind and other living beings of wild life and plants of animal instinct associated with human beings. Hence the solstice of June and solstice of December are turning points of the Earth & the Moon around the Sun. The solstice of summer /winter and the solstice of winter /summer are the course of the Earth's opposite fields that end before equinox of north & south for reproduction extra repulsive forces in the evening hours of new moon period and for reproduction extra impulsive forces with gravitational forces at the end evening moonlight and at the beginning of morning moonlight before equinox quarterly. Therefore, the solstice of winter / summer is the beginning of year quarterly as spring towards summer. The solstice of summer/winter is the beginning of autumn towards winter quarterly for reproduction life cycles opposite magnetic fields of the north & south axis charged by the Sun & the Moon for growing new life plants around Earth specially in the Northern & Southern hemisphere around the Sun. The 1st and 3rd quarter of year are on the Earth's axis of opposite fields that begin as spring & autumn on opposite hemisphere for installation living energy of seven senses of the Sun God & the Moon Goddess into living cells of waterbody in the pot of Mother Moon of the Earth (Woman) in spring of either half of north or south when there is extra magnetic force of the Sun and the Moon with gravitational forces during the full Moon week to form an unit of life made by opposite organism in spring of 1st or 3rd quarter of year to grow in the 2nd or 4th quarter of year in summer of year to mature in autumn of either half of 3rd or 1st quarter of year.

But the winter of 4th or 2nd quarter of year on north or south respectively around equinox or after equinox winter is for releasing super human beings of the Earths opposite halves.

The 4th quarter or 2nd quarter of year is the period of winter on opposite halves for receiving the new value of human life plant in the Northern & Southern hemisphere as humanity. The summer on the southern and northern hemisphere is for installation of new life plant in the pot of Goddess Mother Earth of animal kind of different varieties as animal instinct towards solstice of summer around midday of summer that occur in the month of June & in the month of December on both hemisphere.

So, we humankind must believe that Humankind is philosophic life plants of magnetic fields of the north & south projected by the Sun and the Moon on the Earth's axis of North and South into living cells of waterbody contained into eggs in the alive life-pots of Goddess Mother Earth/ Moon (Woman) for growing live cells of the Sun and the Moon on the Earth according to the positions of the Earth and the Moon around Sun's Northfield six months and Southfield six months following the speed of recycles of rotation and revolution of the Earth and the Moon around the Sun.

Everybody should personify my physical body system of man & woman is separated from the whole-body system of the

Earth/Moon as life partner extended from the Sun as an agent/ person of male & female. Everybody should personify the Sun and the Moon as live energy as a principle of magnetic force of the Earth's opposite fields of the Sun God & the Moon Goddess charged continuously and distributed the same systematically by the recycle of rotation/ revolution of the Earth & the Moon around the Sun God: -

(i)   after solstice as spring & autumn according to the position of the axis of the Earth and Moon around Sun's axis before equinox. After crossing the equinox of March the line of equator on north and the equinox of September the line of equator on South, the Earth's opposite field is towards extreme summer quite opposite to winter; and

(ii)   after equinox, the morning summer during new moon is towards autumn summer and the evening winter is towards spring winter during full moon period on the North or south. From equinox of 22nd / 23rd September to solstice of December and from equinox of 21st / 22nd March to solstice of June are summers for animal instinct and are winters of humankind of humanity.

Therefore, the period of spring & autumn of either half of north or south is the period of conception of woman mother for maintaining peace & harmony in every family of human society. This period is the evening sunlight/ moonlight of the North towards equinox of September is the morning moonlight / sunlight of the southern half. The period from January to equinox of March is autumn of summer of south but it is the spring of winter of northern half for conception live cells of the Lord into eggs of humankind in the alive lifeboats of the Earth/Moon on north & south.

CHAPTER 5

Family Responsibility and the Principle of Replantation

Every family of humankind must realize that to follow the spiritual and scientific creative principle of replantation of living energy of senses of magnetic forces of the Sun and the Moon on the Earth's axis into living cells of waterbody into eggs in the alive lifeboats of Mother Earth/Moon (Woman) is derived from right & left ovaries. The above is the common divine life creative principle of humankind projected by the two opposite fields of the Sun and the Moon on the Earth according to the position of the Earth and the Moon around Sun to the North six months & to the South six months. According to the position of the Earth in between the Sun & the Moon after solstice of summer as autumn towards winter and after solstice of winter as spring towards summer quite opposite on north or south. Every good parent must select the spring of either half for maintaining future generation. According to the theory of recycles of spring & autumn in every family there is chance of incarnation of past souls in the alive life-pots of great Mother Earth/Moon according to the will power of the person of male & female while taking role of parent of the Earth/Moon as there is replantation of XY & XX live cells energy of the Lord into eggs in the alive life-pots of male & female of Mother Earth/Moon.

Every family of humankind must not forget that we two persons of man & woman are the opposite living energy of seven senses of

Sun God projected by the Earth & the Moon at midnight during mature moon week (period) quite the opposite to the Sun's axis on the Earth to grow the living energy of plus and minus of the Sun & the Moon into living cells of waterbody in the life-pots of goddess Mother Earth /Moon (Woman) on north & south.

The Whole-body system of humankind of the Earth's opposite axis are the Man and Woman regulated by the schedule time of the recycles of the Earth and Moon made by the magnetic fields of the Earth & the Moon while revolving around the Sun six months to north and six months to south after every solstice of north & south to complete the process of making two organisms of opposite fields.

Every family of couple of life should realize the fact that we two are life plants growing in the alive lifeboats of Mother Earth /Moon (Woman) on north & south as projected by the magnetic fields of the North and South fields of the Sun and the Moon on the Earth following the recycles of the Earth and the Moon around Sun to the North six months and to the South six months. The 22nd of December and 22nd of June is the turning point from January to 21st March around January/February and from July to 22nd September around July/August. The full moon week in the 1st and 3rd quarter of year respectively are for installing live cells of the Lord into lifeboats of the goddess Mother Moon of the Earth/ Moon to grow in the 2nd or in the 4th quarter of year to sail the lifeboat from equinox to solstice and from solstice to equinox to complete the growing process of opposite organisms of the Earth's opposite fields.

The theme of project work of the magnetic force of the Sun and the Moon around the Earth is the principle of the Lord to be followed by every citizen & family of the people spiritually, scientifically, philosophically, culturally, traditionally, religiously. People settled on north & south fields are responsible to follow as entrusted by the magnetic force of nature. In any case to discharge duties blindly by the people without sufficient knowledge & conscience based on the logic and reasons of data of accounts of north and south magnetic fields of the Earth & the Moon regulated by the Sun & the Moon is harmful to children & family clan and in the society. To work blindly without future plan & hope of the Lord may be good or worse in future life of young generations of opposite halves of nature.

So, we must give proper educations to the children and young people and potential parent. We should never force my opposite young love partner before getting education opposite fields of magnetic fields of the Earth & the Moon regulated by the opposite fields of the Sun & the Moon of the solar system. Humankind is executing the most important duty of life it can give good effects in the life time of both halves. We, two life partners of the Lord should realize each other about the fact & figure of forming magnetic attachment force of the North and South fields of the Earth's axis by the opposite fields of the Sun & the Moon. We must introduce the spring & autumn seasons on north after solstice clockwise and the spring & autumn on south after solstice quarterly. We must also introduce the summer & winter after equinox quarterly in the up journey of life partner of the Earth /Moon through education system, the basic principles of the time recycle of the life earth & the moon in the world. We two living beings in a family of a couple must be well organized in the working system & process jointly to get the fruit of the magnetic force of Godhead on the Earth without any difference of spiritual world as discussed above for the welfare of new life generations of all living beings.

To root out the evil spirit from human society, every family of the Earth & the Moon is projected by the Sun and the Moon in the spring & autumn. We must check our unpleasant bad habits, quarrelling each other; without knowing the common solution for the welfare of human society permanently. Our bad habit of committing crime by the opposite organism as animal instinct to the satisfaction of bad people is seen in the political people in open manner like animals. How it is so harmful to the general society.

Bad characters of people are known by the general people as brought by the political people influenced by very mean thoughts attacking to the main stream of human society developed from many centuries after discussion of thousands of years. Big country swallowed the small states of well-organized people of local region state. To attack the Indigenous people of high culture without seeing the consequences of future generation is so harmful to the people of the world without giving chance of discussion of past history, is whose interest in the present scenario. Who is the authority of the Government that encourage the wild & wrong people to destroy the Manipuri society, after committing the crime to the people of Manipur, who will be benefitted? The wrong doers are the authority of big country who are seeing the reaction of their crime with multiple troubles. In the history of Manipur & big country they are trying to divide among themselves with multiple peaches that can never be united. The big country will be divided into pieces because of the reaction.

We should not discharge any kind of duty against the mainstream of human society who always support the people of the Lord. That the false practice committed by bad people in the past thinking for self of communally is against the benefits of every citizen and that will do more harm to the communal people of the country amongst themselves. Human society is not for communal people but it is for the people human society of humanity spread throughout the world. We must think right & wrong, good, & bad regulated by the light system of the Lord for our future life generations to generation.

CHAPTER 6

Political Leadership and the Magnetic Forces of Nature

In this age of science and technology, the political leaders of Humankind settled in different regions of the World must reorganize as a common platform as a forum to discuss about the magnetic forces of the Sun and the Moon projected on the Earth's opposite axis after solstice as new moon period on one side for both fields for autumn and as full Moon period on another side for both fields as spring season for both fields as spring towards summer and as autumn towards winter. The life cycles of the Earth's opposite halves change directions in the up journey after equinox towards summer on one half and towards winter on another quite opposite on north & south according to inclination of the Earth's axis from the equator line. The life system of short life span of animal kind of different varieties begins without visions of life around the equatorial regions in the land & water of the Earth after equinox of 23rd September on south anticlockwise and after equinox of 21st March on north clockwise as growing process opposite hemispheres as growth living beings/plants. The germination of live cells into eggs in the lifeboats of male & female after equinox of north & south is for animal instinct for starting new life.

Humankind of super beings of humanity is above the animal kind they should board in the lifeboats of male & female into eggs of goddess woman mother of the Earth/Moon who comes from the face of Moon Goddess around the Earth in spring & autumn of either half to sail around the Sun in the ocean of life (i) from 22nd March to September clockwise on north and anticlockwise on south and (ii) from 22nd September to March are conception period for human beings of opposite organism in the womb of Mother Earth/Moon because of declination of the Earth's opposite hemispheres. The lifeboats sailing on opposite hemispheres will release/ deliver as issues of the earth/ moon around equinox of winter of either half. The people of communal instinct of self without solution is like animal instinct.

The 22nd of December, and 21st June solstice of winter/summer is the turning point of life plants for new life recycle growing on the Earth's opposite axis because of the magnetic fields of North and South of the Sun and the Moon on the Earth's axis along with the attractive magnetic forces produced during new moon period and full Moon period quite opposite to the Sun's axis of north & south. The Sun & the Moon contributes high tide into waterbody of the Earth/Moon contained into eggs during the spring & autumn to remove dark shadow of the Earth in the pole regions.

We all should realize the effect of full Moon week period to the humankind life plants growing into living cells of waterbody of the Earth. Every political leader who comes out in the public to serve the people must know the systematic principles of nature for the welfare of people and environment. Every good citizen and parent of the Earth must know the systematic principles of nature and think very deeply about the functions of the earth / the moon and the functions of the Sun / the Moon as great parent to bring a change to the Humankind of the Earth on north / south in brighter future generation as directed by Lord. That policy and program of the Government is to make an institution of systematic principles of nature for the welfare of people. The institution of the Government must be initiated by the senior well educated people selected by every well-educated experienced potential family parent of human society who are recognized by the people of the region as good character person in the history of the region of the state of the Earth. The Earth cannot stand in the environment without the Moon attached as life partner while rotating/revolving around the Sun's axis from north to south six months and from south to north six months for making new policies and programs for the welfare of social science based on spiritual / scientific creative principles of the earth /moon for creation of a new World of Human society of civilization through common platform and principles of wonderful spiritual Magnetic force of the Sun and the Moon charged on the Earth's opposite fields after every solstice of summer & winter of north & south as spring & autumn quite opposite to the Sun's axis of north & south. The longest daytime / nighttime of north/south of summer/winter and south/ north winter/ summer from midnight to noontime summer beginning of the year and from noontime summer to midnight winter is the beginning of evening hours of the year quarterly before equinox of March and before equinox of September on north & south.

We two citizen of man /woman are bound to discharge the bounden duty with obligations from each & every citizen and parent of the Earth/ Moon, as directed by the Sun and the Moon. If we two involve equally to follow the creative principles to the satisfaction of the Lord projected as a unique feature of magnetic force for humankind life plants of the Earth/Moon in time for the welfare of all people and all living beings/plants of the environment of the Earth's opposite halves it is sure we all are protected by the Lord.

CHAPTER 7

Magnetic Forces of the Moon on the Earth

The Moon is towards the Sun during new Moon week and again the Moon is quite opposite to the Sun during full Moon week. The Moon takes 14 days, 12 hours, some minutes, and some seconds when she comes from new Moon to full Moon quite opposite to the Sun at midnight winter/summer during full moon. The Moon takes 14 days, 12 hours, some minutes, and some seconds faster when She comes from full Moon to new Moon following the speed of magnetic force plus gravitational force of the Sun and the Earth from time to time. Therefore, the full Moon week of spring / autumn of three lunar months of either field is the best period of transformation of XY live cells of the opposite fields of the North & south of the Lord into XX cells contained in the eggs of the Goddess Mother of the Earth/Moon (woman) before equinox due the inclination of the Earth's axis around January/February before March or around July/August before September equinox.

This is the history of growth of life cycles of living beings/ plants of super human beings regulated by the magnetic forces of the Lord played by the Sun & the Moon around the Earth (man) & the Moon (woman) that contributes to grow living cells of the Lord into live cells of waterbody in the eggs of great Goddess Mother Earth/ Moon (Woman) during full Moon week (period) in every family of the Earth/ Moon. The germination of living energy of the Sun God into living cells of waterbody with magnetic forces of the Earth/ Moon occur only when the Earth is in between the Sun and the Moon after solstice in spring/ autumn of either field.

The development of opposite magnetic force of the Moon around the Earth matures when the Moon reaches in the West sky from 12th to 18th days of lunar month quite opposite to the Sun. The growth of opposite magnetic force of north / south expires when the Moon comes to the East sky towards Sun at noontime summer according to the position of the Moon in between the Sun & the Earth in every lunar month.

Therefore, the Moon revolves around the Earth to reproduce opposite magnetic force of the Sun during full Moon week (period) for growing living energy of senses of the Sun God into living cells of waterbody in the pot of Goddess Mother Earth represented by (Woman).

While revolving around the Earth, the Moon contributes attractive opposite magnetic force with gravitational force in the life-pots of Goddess Mother Earth/ Moon (Woman) during full

Moon week quite the opposite to the Sun with high tides into waterbody of the Earth. The Woman's function is following the speed of rotation/revolution according to the position of the Earth (Man) and the Moon (Woman) around the Sun to the North six months and to the South six months. Therefore, Earth/Moon at midnight winter/summer produce the spring / autumn on either field before equinox to germinate and to grow up after equinox journey of life cycles. Therefore, Humankind life plants grow on the Earth as issues of the Sun and Moon following the speed of magnetic force of rotation/ revolution of the Earth/ Moon around Sun's axis for projection of magnetic force of the Sun and the Moon on the Earth during full Moon week period when the Earth is in between the North or South fields of the Sun & the Moon six monthlies after solstice.

CHAPTER 8

The Spiritual and Scientific Principles of Creation

Therefore, Humankind have been organizing a perfectly balance family partners of two opposite Poles of the Earth / Moon to project the life plants of magnetic force of the Sun and the Moon on the Earth in time following the recycle of the Earth and the Moon around Sun to the North six months & to the South six months. To grow life plants of the Earth's opposite fields is according to position of North Pole of the Sun facing towards South Pole of the Earth starting from 22nd December a turning point for new life plant cycle of the Earth's opposite halves around the Sun to keep record of history of past, present and future on the Earth since from the inception of humankind life plant of the Earth. This is a fact according to formula of magnetic force of North and South Poles of the Earth and Moon around Sun God.

Especially important Note of Humankind:

This is a fact on the Earth that the recycle of today on the Earth's north & south has its turning point as 24.00 hours in a day on north & south. The noon & midnight are the ends & beginning of morning & evening hours of year. The morning and evening hours of year begins today at midnight & noon quite opposite on north & south after solstice. In the same way, the recycle of new moon & the full

Moon period are for union of opposite fields that begins during full Moon week (period) for production opposite negative living cells of magnetic fields of the Earth/Moon that begins quite opposite to the Sun & Moon after winter solstice as morning moonlight of the lunar month for three months as spring & autumn before equinox and as summer & winter of three months as the living energy of senses of two opposite halves before solstice. The negative cells of the opposite halves expire when the opposite magnetic force loss on the Earth towards the Sun due to the position of the Moon on the Earth towards the Sun as new moon. The life is the recycle of opposite living cells of magnetic force developed in the lifeboats of male & female in the eggs of the Mother Earth/ Moon (Woman) as history of cycle of Moon designed in the past, on opposite halves for present life system of the Earth and the present positions of the two opposite fields united at midnight winter/summer is for future generation of tomorrow.

The growing process of negative cells of waterbody of Mother Earth (Woman) depending to the position of the Moon of the Earth around Sun to the North and South after solstice as autumn & spring and as spring & autumn. Hence the recycle of evening & morning hours of year is related on opposite axis of the Earth on north & south as the source of energy of the Sun & the Moon for human life plants' as life cycles of magnetic fields of the Earth & the Moon regulated by the Sun after solstice.

But it has its turning point in every 365 days for adding six hours four times for adding one extra day in every four years in February as 29 days as leap year. The turning point of life plants' cycle of the Earth falls on 22nd December every year and the spiritual magnetic force for projection of new humankind life plants in the alive pot of Mother Earth is projected by the Sun and the Moon on the Earth's axis during full Moon week lunar monthly for three months quarterly in the 1st and quarterly in the 3rd quarter of year to germinate in spring/autumn before equinox and grow the lifeboats of male & female quite opposite on north clockwise and on south anticlockwise before equinox. After equinox of north or south the lifeboats change their respective direction in the 2nd and again in the 4th quarter of year for enabling to reproduce the new life plants cycles of male & female of the Earth's opposite fields around equinox of September in the 4th and around equinox of March on opposite hemispheres in the 2nd quarter year. According to recycle of magnetic force of the Sun and Moon on the Earth's axis the Earth/Moon keep history of life cycles of the past for present and life cycles of the present as history for future life plants of new generations. The scenario of human society of today is product of the past as regulated by midday & midnight of opposite hemispheres by the sun in the east & by the moon at midnight after every solstice of north & south in summer & winter.

CHAPTER 9

Violation of Natural Law and the Disorder of Humankind

The root cause of coming the present scenario of disorder of humankind of man & woman on the Earth is the cause of violation of the basic principle of creation of humankind life plant by the parents: due to lack of the knowledge, obedience, and obeisance to the Godfather & Goddess Mother of the people of the Lord. The blindness of human service by an individual as a citizen and by a parent representing the Earth & the Moon is related against the light system of the Sun and the Moon directed by the Lord of the solar system and other talented stars around the galaxy of the universe. The cycle of time of today is at midnight hour for growing up by installing the living energy of seven senses of the Sun God into living cells of waterbody present in the alive pot of great Goddess Mother Moon of the Earth (Woman).

The recycle of time of year for growing positive magnetic force of the Earth is from 23rd December to 21st March and from 22nd June to 22nd September to start from the 1st & 3rd quarter of year to grow on opposite halves and to release on opposite half in the 2nd & 4th quarter of year and to complete the growing process of opposite fields in the 3rd or 1st quarter of year in the autumn seasons of either half as babies / offspring of the Earth/Moon around equinox in the 4th or 2nd quarter of year on opposite fields as wish by the Godhead.

The recycle of Full Moon week (12th to 18th days) have been developed at midnight winter/ summer around Earth's axis of north & south quite the opposite to the Sun for developing opposite attractive (positive) and distractive (negative) magnetic forces of the North & South fields of the Sun & the Moon around the Earth's axis during the full Moon week in the negative cells of waterbody in the alive lifeboats of Goddess Mother Moon (Woman) of Earth when the Earth's opposite fields are in between the Sun & the Moon in spring/ autumn seasons of north & south.

So, we, potential father and mother living in a well- organized family of humankind of the Earth & the Moon should modify and correct the principle and procedures of plantation of living energy of seven senses of the Sun God into living cells of waterbody of magnetic force in the pot of great Goddess Mother of the Earth/Moon (Woman) during full Moon week when projected by the Sun & Moon in the 1st or 3rd quarter to present the right new life plants of the Earth in the 4th or 2nd quarter of year on opposite fields as a responsible father and mother of humankind for the welfare of all people and environment of the Earth.

This program and policy of Humankind should be introduced on the Earth as unique feature of magnetic force of the Sun and Moon during full Moon week (period) at midnight hour when the Moon is quite opposite to the Sun the Moon reflect the seven senses of sunlight as rainbow into living cells of waterbody contained in the eggs of Mother Earth/Moon (produced by Woman mother) in the 1st & 3rd quarter of year in spring /autumn to present the new life plants of humankind around the equinox in the 4th & 2nd quarter of year. The act of today of humankind life plants under certain principle will bring the fruit of future of today of people would be the principle of past for present as the root cause of coming the status of future generation of human society of today.

Violation of Natural Law and the Disorder of Humankind

The present crisis and problem of humankind seems to have been missing the original principle of creation human life plants of humankind of the earth's opposite halves projected by the Sun and the Moon in time in spring & autumn of either north & south.

On the other Side, according to the position of the Earth's axis around the North Pole & the South Pole of the Sun God, the Earth receives positive magnetic force of living energy from the Northern half of the Sun towards Southern field of the Earth/Moon and from Southern field of the Sun, towards northern field of the Earth/ Moon due to the inclination of the Earth (man) and the

Moon (Woman) around the Sun's axis. The North and South fields of the Earth have been absorbing the magnetic force of the Sun's axis for six months from 23rd September to 21st March and from 22nd March to 22nd September. The North & South field of the Earth's axis have been absorbing extra magnetic forces from the Sun & the Moon after solstice towards equinox as spring in the morning 12 hours & as autumn in the evening 12 hours due to inclination of the Earth's opposite fields from the Sun for three months for creation of super human beings of the Sun & the Moon on the Earth/Moon. During this period, the negative field of Earth absorbed the positive magnetic field from the Sun God on one side and on the other side the negative field of the Earth/ Moon absorbed the positive magnetic field of the Moon at midnight winter/ summer during full Moon week in the morning 12 hours of two weeks lunar monthly from the Moon when the Earth is in between the Sun and the Moon after solstice of north & south six monthlies.

Therefore, in this age of science and technology of magnetic force of opposite fields played by the Lord, human kind can realize that humankind life plants are growing into the living cells of waterbody contained in the eggs of the Mother Earth/ Moon (Woman) as male & female lifeboats as projected by the magnetic fields of the Sun and the Moon as eggs into XX cells in the alive lifeboats of Goddess Mother woman produced from the right & left ovaries of two opposite axis of the Earth.

We should realize that the magnetic force of seven senses of the Sun God and Moon Goddess is absorbed by the Southern and the Northern fields of the Earth as a unique feature during the full Moon period in spring & autumn as a principle of creation of humankind for growing into living cells of waterbody in the pot of Mother Woman of the earth. We two persons must realize that the attractive magnetic forces of the Northern and Southern fields of the Earth & the Moon are produced during the full Moon week in spring & autumn period. So, this period of spring & autumn of opposite fields is the best period for germination of living energy of senses of Sun God / the Moon Goddess into living cells of waterbody of the woman Mother Earth/ Moon projected by the magnetic fields of the Sun and the Moon on the Earth for creation of Humankind, as the most important life plant of the great Goddess Mother Earth (Woman).

Do you want to follow the philosophic principles of the Sun and the Moon projected into living cells of waterbody produced by the eggs of the great Goddess Mother Earth (Woman) in the spring season before equinox in order to see the real fruits of magnetic fields of the Lord as life plant of man & woman as male & female in spring & autumn season on the Earth or not?

If the reply is 'yes' it is ok, we all are equal living beings as citizen of opposite fields under certain principle of the Earth & the Moon as life partner. If the reply is 'no' what is your philosophic principles to support your reply and if you cannot give your reply supported by reasons you have been separated as evil spirit as working against the magnetic fields of two opposite fields of the mass bodies present in the space world of different mass bodies well settled on their respective orbits as regulated by magnetic force of North and South Poles and gravitational forces of the axis of the mass bodies of the Universe cause continuous rotation / revolution of the mass bodies of the space on their orbits around the sun with logic and reasons.

The Moon follows the speed of rotation of the Earth's axis and the speed of revolution of the Earth's axis around the Sun's axis to the North from 23rd September to 21st March and during this period the Earth is around extreme North of the Sun on the 22nd of December with attractive magnetic force of the Earth.

While revolving around the Sun's axis of north field six months and of south field six months, the Moon follows the speed of rotation/ revolution of the Earth's axis from new Moon to the full Moon and from full Moon to new Moon.

The Moon contributes magnetic force producing living cells of waterbody in the pot of great Goddess Mother Earth (Woman) during full Moon week. The magnetic force of the Sun and the Moon contribute to germinate living energy of the Sun God into living cells of waterbody present in the pot of Goddess Mother Earth (Woman) at midnight hour when the Earth is in between the Sun and the Moon in the 1st quarter of year.

The great Goddess Mother Earth (Woman) takes 9 months to construct the complete structure of life plants of humankind growing in the living pot of great Mother Earth (Woman). The great Mother Earth (Woman) releases the life plants of humankind on the Earth in the 4th quarter of year from 23rd September to 22nd December.

The full Moon week period from 12th to 18th day around the Earth is quite opposite to the Sun and the Moon reflects the beams of Sunlight with attractive (negative) magnetic force towards the Northern half from West sky producing living cells of waterbody in the pot of Mother Earth (Woman) with high tide at midnight hour according to the position of the Earth and Moon around the Sun God.

This principle of full Moon week period contributes the growth of living cells of waterbody of life plants of Humankind growing in the pot of Mother Earth (Woman) as a project work of the Sun and the Moon on the Earth according to the position of the Sun and the

Moon around Sun as a spring season for installing new life plant on the Earth.

Under the same principle, the Earth and the Moon revolve around the Sun to the North for six months and again to the South for six months after every solstice. According to the position of the Earth and Moon around Sun's axis contributes positive and negative magnetic field of the North towards the Southern half and again of the South towards Northern half around the Earth for every six months from one equinox to another equinox.

This fact of relationship of magnetic fields of the Sun and the Moon around the Earth's axis is proved by the projection of Sunlight from the North inclining towards the South and again from the South inclining towards the North during the full Moon week period quite opposite to the Sun God. The Moon goddess contributes this service to the living cells of waterbody present in the pot of Mother Earth /Moon (Woman) on north & south lunar monthly for three months as spring & autumn on opposite fields before 23rd September equinox and before 21st March equinox of spring quite the opposite on the south & north for growing life plants of the Sun & the Moon in the pot of Mother Earth / Moon to support Humankind life plants projected by the Sun and the Moon in the 1st & the 3rd quarter of year to complete growing process of opposite fields in the 4th quarter of year on north and in the 2nd quarter of year on south.

The principle of projection of positive & negative magnetic fields of the Sun & the Moon on the Earth's opposite fields begins from 23rd December to 21st March and again from 22nd June to 22nd September according to the position of the Earth and the Moon to the Northfield of the Sun six months and to the Southfield of the Sun six months. During the period, the Moon projects the Sunlight with magnetic force quite the opposite to the Sun during full Moon week into living cells of waterbody present in the pot of Mother Earth /Moon (Woman) on north & south as spring & autumn for germination of living energy of the Sun God with magnetic force of the Sun and the Moon on the Earth at midnight hour to grow the same as life plant of living beings in the pot of Mother Earth /Moon (Woman) following the recycle of rotation and revolution of the Earth & the Moon around the Sun's axis.

The life plants of Humankind so projected during full Moon week is the real issue of great Godfather and Goddess Mother Earth and the real issue of the Sun and the Moon projected on the Earth's axis. If the parent of the Earth & the Moon, follow the time recycles of the Earth & the Moon around the Sun's axis for the new offspring of the man & woman. It is the real issue of great God father Earth and the Goddess Mother Moon of the Earth and humankind call the persons as "king & queen of the Earth" and give the title of "Pakhangba" to the Son & daughter of the Lord who comes on the Earth.

"Pakhangba" means the person of living plant of humankind who knows the Godfather Earth & Goddess Mother Moon projected by the Sun & the Moon in the solar system while orbiting in the galaxy of the universe.

The person produced under strict time recycles of the Earth & the Moon is called the "Pakhangba" growing into living cells of waterbody born from the living pot of great Goddess Mother Earth. The Sun God is the eldest Son of Godhead the living energy of seven senses of light system present to every life plant of Humankind and animal kind is growing into living cells of waterbody present in the pot of Mother Earth and to the persons of every Woman and other female mothers present in every house of people of the Earth & the Moon organized as human society of the Earth. Every man & woman is the image of the king of God and queen of Goddess "Lainingthou" is the image of the Lord having two opposite fields of the Earth, and of the Moon regulated by the two opposite fields of the Sun's axis and other opposite fields of space mass bodies of eight planets & satellites of the solar system as directed by the Lord. We can achieve the spiritual power of the Lord by praying to the Lord by way of meditation about the systematic principles of the World of life plants of humankind and other animal kind growing on the Earth and that the other life plants of the environment support the humankind on the Earth.

According to Manipuri custom, tradition, and religion, "Pakhangba" is the king of humankind who rules other living beings/ plants and other animal kinds of this environment. Humankind is the youngest issue of Godhead who rules the living beings of the Earth & the Moon. We call the energy as the king of God and queen of Goddess who is shining as the Sun God & the Moon Goddess. According to Manipuri language, we call God as "Lai" and the king as "Ningthou". We call the king of God & Goddess as "Lainingthou" and the Godhead represent the Sun God & others space mass bodies. When "Lainingthou" is present in our person we call the live energy as "Lainingthou Sanamahi". According to Manipuri tradition, custom, culture, and religion of Manipuri lifestyle, we worship the king of God, equal to Godhead as "Lainingthou" inside every person & house as home of Lord.

We keep a place reserved for king of God in our dwelling house in the South/West corner of the house reserved for "Lainingthou". We believe that creation of humankind life plant is done by the Sun God and the Moon Goddess on the Earth from the Southwest corner of the Home at midnight for going towards Northeast corner and the energy of the Lord is returning from Northeast corner towards Southwest corner for completing after every solstice quite opposite to the axis of the Earth of new moon as autumn towards equinox at beginning of winter.

According to our Manipuri custom, culture, & tradition as religion, of Sanamahism we cannot do anything without His permission & blessing from "Lainingthou Sanamahi". Because of this reason for any service on the stage of Earth, we take blessing from "Lainingthou" present in the home of my person for enabling to discharge of duty of life in the most important bounden duty for creation of new life generation of future at midnight winter/ summer of today extended in spring & autumn on either half as directed by the Sun & the Moon at noontime summer and at midnight winter for the welfare of people around the Earth in every family in the environment of the Earth's north & south as projected by the Lord after every solstice to humankind of the Earth/Moon.

The cycle of the moon controlled the menstruation cycle of moon of the earth. The menstruation cycle of woman mother is also controlled by the cycle of the whole moon period around the earth at noon time summer and midnight time winter as new moon week. The production of live cells and death cells by woman mother is a continuous process controlled by the whole moon period comprising of 28 to 29 days. The role of the moon is for woman of the earth. Everybody who is coming on the earth is under the process of production of egg cells produced from the right and left ovaries of the woman mother and everyone of male and female of the earth depends to the woman mother earth projected by the sun and moon after every solstice. Every animal kind of living beings are also controlled by the living cells produced by the sun and moon after equinox of March and September in the summer season. If we don't care, respect and honor the functions of the mother earth played by the woman mother, we cannot enjoy life of humanity formed by the love and attachment of opposite fields of the earth and moon regulated by the sun.

Let God bless everyone on the Earth on the North & South of the Earth.

APPENDIX

Explanation of Key Terms

Solstice

A solstice is the turning point of the year when the Earth reaches its maximum tilt toward or away from the Sun. It occurs twice annually, around 21st June and 22nd December.

In June, one hemisphere experiences the longest day of the year, while the opposite hemisphere experiences the longest night. In December, the condition reverses.

In the context of this book, the solstice represents more than an astronomical event. It marks a symbolic transition in the cycle of energy between the Northern and Southern hemispheres. It is described as a point of renewal, where the directional flow of seasonal and magnetic influence begins to shift.

Equinox

An equinox occurs twice each year, around 21st March and 22nd September, when day and night are nearly equal in length across the Earth.

At this time, the Earth's axis is neither tilted toward nor away from the Sun. Both hemispheres receive nearly equal sunlight.

Within the philosophical framework of this book, the equinox represents balance and crossing. It is seen as a moment when opposing forces—light and darkness, North and South—stand in equilibrium before continuing their respective seasonal journeys.

Magnetic Fields

Magnetic fields refer to invisible forces generated by celestial bodies such as the Earth and the Sun. Scientifically, the Earth's magnetic field arises from movements within its molten core, while the Sun produces powerful magnetic activity through solar dynamics.

In this work, magnetic fields are used both scientifically and symbolically. They represent attraction and repulsion, positive and negative forces, and the interaction between celestial bodies. The author connects these forces to cycles of life, growth, and transformation, presenting them as governing principles within the natural order.

Spring and Autumn Cycle

Spring and autumn are transitional seasons that follow solstice periods and move toward equinox balance.

Spring symbolizes renewal, emergence, and preparation for growth. Autumn symbolizes maturity, transformation, and preparation for rest.

In this book, these seasons are interpreted as key phases in the broader cosmic rhythm. They are presented as periods of intensified interaction between the Earth and the Moon, symbolizing regeneration and continuity within the cycle of life.

Full Moon Week

The full moon occurs when the Earth stands between the Sun and the Moon, allowing the Moon's surface to be fully illuminated from Earth's perspective.

The "full Moon week," as described in this book, refers to the days surrounding the full moon phase, typically between the 12th and 18th lunar days. During this period, gravitational forces between the Earth, Moon, and Sun are aligned in a way that influences tides and natural rhythms.

In the author's philosophical interpretation, this phase represents heightened energetic interaction and symbolic union of opposing forces. It is treated as a significant period within the recurring cycle of natural processes.

FURTHER READING & REFLECTION

Readers who wish to explore these ideas in greater depth may consult the author's earlier work, *The Secrets of Life (The Only Solution of Life)* by Waikhom Bhumeswar Singh, Advocate.

Additional explanations and visual presentations are available through the author's public platforms, including the video series *Century Life Calendar (An Infallible Guide – Parts 1, 2, 3, and 4)* available on YouTube.

Hard copies of the author's books are available in major libraries such as the National Library in Kolkata, the Central Library in Imphal, and public libraries in Mumbai, Chennai, and New Delhi, as well as leading bookstores in Imphal and Guwahati. The books are also accessible worldwide in Kindle edition through Amazon.

The author encourages readers not to accept any belief blindly. Human understanding evolves, and traditions shaped by time and place may carry limitations. Since human life is brief and the world changes continuously, it is essential to seek truth through thoughtful reflection and independent inquiry.

Life unfolds through natural cycles of birth, growth, maturity, and renewal, guided by the order expressed in nature. True understanding arises from logic, reason, and careful observation of natural law.

Logic and reason remain the foundation of human philosophy and the path toward responsible and balanced living.

www.ingramcontent.com/pod-product-compliance
Lightning Source LLC
Chambersburg PA
CBHW052121150726
48002CB00006B/2439